500 THINGS
MY DOG TOLD ME

Published by USA BOOKS, INC.

Send all inquiries to: USA BOOKS, INC., PO BOX 51524, Sarasota, Florida, 34232

1. WOOF!

2. A DOG CAN EXPRESS MORE WITH HIS TAIL IN A MINUTE THAN HIS OWNER CAN EXPRESS WITH HIS TONGUE IN AN HOUR.

3. IF YOUR DOG IS FAT, IT MEANS THAT YOU AREN'T GETTING ENOUGH EXERCISE.

4. LIFE IS JUST ONE TABLE SCRAP AFTER ANOTHER!

5. IGLOO WAS A FOX TERRIER WHO TRAVELED WITH ADMIRAL BYRD ON FLIGHTS OVER THE NORTH AND SOUTH POLES. NO ONE KNOWS IF HIS NAME WAS DUE TO COINCIDENCE OR AMAZING FORESIGHT.

6. SO MANY SHOES - SO LITTLE TIME!

7. DOGS WERE THE FIRST ANIMALS TO BE TAMED BY MAN. WHAT CAN I SAY? WE'RE EASY.

8. TO ERR IS HUMAN - TO FORGIVE IS CANINE.

3

9. IF YOU HAVE INSOMNIA, TRY TURNING AROUND IN CIRCLES A FEW TIMES BEFORE YOU LIE DOWN. IT WORKS FOR US.

10. YOU ACTUALLY CAN TEACH AN OLD DOG NEW TRICKS... BUT THAT DOESN'T MEAN HE'LL DO THEM.

11. FEED ME!

12. RIN-TIN-TIN HATED HIS NAME.

13. IT'S ALWAYS BEST TO LET A SLEEPING DOG LIE. ESPECIALLY WHEN HE'S RIGHT IN THE MIDDLE OF YOUR BED.

14. THERE IS NO SUCH THING AS "BAD FOOD."

15. FRANZ KAFKA ONCE SAID, "ALL KNOWL-EDGE, THE TOTALITY OF ALL QUESTIONS AND ALL ANSWERS, IS CONTAINED IN THE DOG." THEN HE TURNED INTO A BUG OF SOME SORT AND WAS NEVER HEARD FROM AGAIN.

16. EVEN THE TINIEST DOG IS A WOLF AT HEART.

5

17. THAT WAS A LONG WALK - BOY, ARE MY DOGS BARKIN'!

18. JUST A LITTLE DOG HUMOR, THERE.

19. OVER EIGHT THOUSAND DOGS SERVED IN THE "K9 CORPS" OF THE UNITED STATES ARMY DURING WORLD WAR II. SEE - WE CAN BE PATRIOTIC, TOO!

20. WHOEVER SAID THAT MONEY CAN'T BUY HAPPINESS OBVIOUSLY FORGOT ABOUT PUPPIES.

21. I PROMISE NOT TO BARK AT THE ANSWERING MACHINE.

22. NO DOG IS TOO PROUD TO BEG - PARTICULARLY WHEN YOU'RE HAVING STEAK FOR DINNER.

23. ONE OF THE REASONS DOGS ARE SO LOVABLE IS THAT WE WAG OUR TAILS, NOT OUR TONGUES.

24. I'M NOT FAT - I'M HUSKY!

25. YOU KNOW YOUR DOG IS IN CHARGE IF YOU HAD TO BUY A BIGGER BED JUST SO YOUR DOG COULD HAVE MORE LEG ROOM.

26. I SHED, THEREFORE I AM.

27. WANNA SEE A DOG AND PONY SHOW? ALL WE NEED IS A PONY!

28. YOU CALL IT CHASING ME. I CALL IT EXERCISING YOU. IT'S ALL IN THE PERSPECTIVE.

29. JUST GIVE ME FIVE MINUTES ALONE WITH THE GUY WHO INVENTED THE "CHOKE CHAIN."

30. BARRY, A SAINT BERNARD, RESCUED FORTY PEOPLE WHO GOT LOST IN THE SNOW IN SWITZERLAND'S SAINT BERNARD PASS IN THE YEAR 1800. NOW, THAT'S WHAT I CALL A COINCIDENCE!

31. I'LL TRY TO REMEM-BER: THE CAT IS NOT A TOY.

32. IF YOU WANT THE BEST SEAT IN THE HOUSE, YOU'RE PROBABLY GOING TO HAVE TO MOVE YOUR DOG.

33. EVERY DOG HAS HIS DAY. I WANT MINE NOW!

34. WE'RE STURDY ANIMALS. TRY GETTING EIGHT CATS TO PULL A SLED THROUGH THE SNOW!

35. MY BARK IS WORSE THAN MY BITE.

36. NO, REALLY!

37. YOU PEOPLE INVENT POLLUTION, AND YOU THINK DOGS ARE DUMB?

38. DOGS WILL NEVER MAKE GOOD ASTRO-NAUTS. WE CAN'T STICK OUR HEADS OUT THE WINDOW.

39. THE POINTER DOESN'T ACTUALLY POINT, HE JUST LOOKS IN THE GENERAL DIRECTION OF HIS OWNER'S PREY. WE DON'T WANT TO MAKE IT TOO EASY FOR THE HUNTERS.

40. YES! THE MAILMAN'S HERE!

41. AN ESKIMO DOG NAMED BALTO LED A DOG TEAM THAT CARRIED DIPHTHERIA SERUM SIX HUNDRED MILES THROUGH AN ALASKAN BLIZZARD IN 1925. YOU WOULDN'T FIND ANY CATS DOING THAT SORT OF THING!

42. YOU'RE GETTING ME A CHEW TOY? WHY? I'VE ALREADY GOT THESE SHOES!

43. I PROMISE NOT TO BARK AT THE GARDEN HOSE.

44. I HAVE NO IDEA HOW ALL OF THAT DOG HAIR GOT IN THE FISH POND.

45. WE DON'T LIKE "DOGGIE DOORS." THEY TAKE AWAY OUR ABILITY TO ANNOY YOU IN THE MIDDLE OF THE NIGHT.

46. THERE IS NO SUCH THING AS A "BAD DOG BISCUIT."

47. WELL, IF YOU'D PUT YOUR DINNER ON THE FLOOR, I WOULDN'T HAVE TO STAND HERE AND BEG FOR IT, WOULD I?

48. ROLLING AROUND IN A MUDDY STREAM SURE SEEMS LIKE A GOOD ENOUGH BATH FOR US!

49. HAS ANYONE EVER ACTUALLY HEARD A DOG SAY "BOW-WOW?"

50. IN DOG YEARS, YOU'RE PROBABLY DEAD.

51. I ONCE KNEW A DYSLEXIC, AGNOSTIC, INSOMNIAC TERRIER WHO STAYED UP ALL NIGHT WONDERING IF THERE REALLY IS A DOG.

52. A DOG IS ONLY AS MEAN AS HIS OWNER.

15

53. I LOVE YOU, YOU KNOW.

54. BULLDOGS WERE ORIGINALLY BRED TO FIGHT BULLS. THAT DIDN'T LAST VERY LONG.

55. DOGGY BREATH: OUR GREATEST EMBARRASSMENT.

56. DO BLIND DOGS HAVE SEEING-EYE PEOPLE?

57. I PROMISE NOT TO BARK AT THE LAUNDRY.

58. OH-OH... LOOKS LIKE I'M IN THE DOGHOUSE AGAIN.

59. IN A PERFECT WORLD, EVERY DOG WOULD HAVE A HOME, AND EVERY HOME WOULD HAVE A DOG.

17

60. SOME DAYS YOU'RE THE DOG, SOME DAYS YOU'RE THE HYDRANT.

61. RHODESIAN RIDGEBACKS HAVE A RIDGE OF FUR ON THEIR BACK THAT RUNS IN THE OPPOSITE DIRECTION FROM THE REST OF THEIR COAT. THAT'S ONE DOG YOU CAN'T RUB THE WRONG WAY!

62. A DOG DOESN'T HAVE TO BE YOUR WHOLE LIFE TO MAKE YOUR LIFE WHOLE.

63. I AM NOT BARKING UP THE WRONG TREE!

64. PAUL MCCARTNEY ADDED AN ULTRA-SONIC WHISTLE, AUDIBLE ONLY TO DOGS, AT THE END OF THE BEATLES' SONG, "A DAY IN THE LIFE," FOR HIS SHETLAND SHEEPDOG. NOW, THAT'S LOVE.

65. THE KING OF CONNACHT IN IRELAND ONCE OFFERED SIX THOUSAND COWS FOR A DOG NAMED AIBE, A WOLFHOUND FAMED FOR HIS HUNTING ABILITY. NO ONE KNOWS WHETHER HE OFFERED THE COWS TO AIBE OR HIS OWNER.

66. I LAUGH WITH MY TAIL.

67. THE "DOG DAYS" OF SUMMER? THAT'S A GOOD THING, RIGHT?

68. THE FAITHFULNESS OF A DOG IS A GIFT TO BE CHERISHED.

69. A LITTLE HEAD TILT GOES A LONG WAY!

70. DOGGONE IT!

71. OKAY, I PROMISE NOT TO EAT THE CAT'S FOOD ANYMORE. CAN I JUST EAT THE CAT?

72. JUST KIDDING!

73. IF PROPERLY TRAINED, A MAN CAN BE A DOG'S BEST FRIEND.

21

74. YOU KNOW YOUR DOG IS IN CHARGE IF YOUR BEDROOM DOOR HAS A DOGGIE DOOR.

75. A GERMAN SHEPHERD NAMED BUDDY BECAME THE FIRST SEEING-EYE DOG, IN THE YEAR 1928.

76. WHIPPETS ALWAYS THINK THEY'RE TOO FAT.

77. YOU MEAN, I HAVE TO SHAKE THE RAIN OFF BEFORE I COME IN THE HOUSE?

78. THERE IS NO SUCH THING AS A "BAD TABLE SCRAP."

79. THERE'S NO SNOOZE BUTTON ON A HUNGRY DOG.

78. A DOG WILL NEVER
BITE WHEN A SIMPLE
GROWL WILL DO.

23

81. SORRY ABOUT ALL THE HOLES, BUT I KNOW THERE'S A BONE BURIED IN THIS YARD SOMEWHERE!

82. HEY! I WAS ON THE BED FIRST!

83. IT'S RAINING CATS AND DOGS? NEAT!

84. AT LEAST WE DON'T DECORATE OUR DOG HOUSES WITH PAINTINGS OF YOU PLAYING POKER.

85. DON'T CLEAN THAT UP - I WAS SAVING IT FOR LATER!

86. DANES ARE GREAT, AREN'T THEY?

87. SOME DOGS CAN
ACTUALLY TELL WHEN
THEIR OWNER IS
ABOUT TO HAVE A
SEIZURE. IS THERE
NO LIMIT TO OUR CAP-
ABILITIES?

88. LOVE ME, LOVE MY OWNER.

89. OR ELSE.

90. MAN. I'M SICK AS A DOG.

91. THERE WAS ONCE A WELSH FOXHOUND THAT GAVE BIRTH TO TWENTY-THREE PUPPIES IN ONE LITTER. SHE SPENT THE REST OF HER LIFE BITING ANY MALE DOG THAT DARED TO COME NEAR HER.

92. HEY, THE CAT STARTED IT!

93. "PUPPY LOVE" IS QUITE REAL - TO A PUPPY.

94. IF YOU THINK DOGS CAN'T COUNT, TRY PUTTING THREE DOG BISCUITS IN YOUR POCKET AND THEN GIVING ME ONLY TWO OF THEM.

27

95. GERMAN SHEPHERDS KNOW THEY'RE COOL.

96. I PROMISE NOT TO BARK AT PAINTINGS OF CATS.

97. EVERY BOY SHOULD HAVE TWO THINGS: A DOG, AND A MOTHER WILLING TO LET HIM HAVE ONE.

98. DOGS ARE JUST BIG HEARTS WITH PAWS.

99. A DOG IS JUST AS HAPPY WITH A POOR FAMILY AS WITH A RICH ONE.

100. SNIFF, SNIFF... HEY, FIDO'S BACK IN TOWN! AND HE HAD A BURRITO FOR LUNCH!

101. IF YOU'VE GONE TO THE DOGS, AT LEAST YOU'LL BE IN GOOD COMPANY.

29

102. I'M GLAD THE POSTMAN ALWAYS RINGS TWICE. IT GIVES US TIME TO PLOT A STRATEGY.

103. THE ROLLED-UP NEWSPAPER: OUR MORTAL ENEMY.

104. WELL, YOU'D BE AS MEAN AS A JUNKYARD DOG IF YOUR HOUSE WAS THAT MESSY, TOO.

105. FEED ME AGAIN!

106. TEARING UP THE FLOOR BOARDS ANNOYS YOU?

107. WHY DOESN'T THE GOVERNMENT DO SOMETHING ABOUT MANGE?

108. YES, I WAS PLANNING
TO WHINE ALL NIGHT
LONG FOR NO
REASON WHATSO-
EVER.   WHY?

31

109. HEY! YOU PUT BLUE STUFF IN MY WATER DISH!

110. WHAT DO YOU MEAN, THAT'S NOT MY WATER DISH?

111. WHY DO I CHASE CARS? BECAUSE THEY'RE THERE.

112. AWW... I DON'T WANNA GO TO OBEDIENCE SCHOOL TODAY!

113. BLOODHOUNDS OCCASIONALLY LEAD THEIR OWNERS TO THE LOCAL BLOOD BANK, JUST FOR KICKS.

114. I AM HOUSEBROKEN. I JUST FORGOT.

115. HISTORY IS FILLED MORE WITH THE LOYALTY OF DOGS THAN OF FRIENDS.

33

116. DOGS LOVE ATTENTION ALMOST AS MUCH AS WE LOVE FOOD.

117. I SAID *ALMOST.*

118. THESE SLIPPERS NEVER LOOKED GOOD ON YOU, ANYWAY.

119. I PROMISE NOT TO BARK AT THE TWINKLY CHRISTMAS LIGHTS.

120. THERE'S ONLY ONE SMARTEST DOG IN THE WORLD - AND EVERY BOY HAS HIM.

121. YOU CAN'T KEEP A GOOD MAN DOWN. THIS ALSO APPLIES TO EXTREMELY AFFECTIONATE DOGS.

122. TIME SPENT WITH DOGS IS NEVER WASTED.

35

123. BOXERS HATE IT WHEN YOU PUT THOSE BIG GLOVES ON THEIR PAWS.

124. YOU LUCKY DOG!

125. YOU KNOW YOUR DOG IS IN CHARGE IF YOU SPEND MORE TIME PREPARING HIS DINNER THAN YOUR OWN.

126. OPEN THE DOOR - I WANT OUT!

127. OPEN THE DOOR - I WANT IN!

128. NOT ONLY DO I NOT MIND WHEN YOU MAKE A FOOL OUT OF YOURSELF - I'M USUALLY INCLINED TO JOIN IN!

_129._ IT'S IMPOSSIBLE TO KEEP A STRAIGHT FACE IN THE PRESENCE OF A PUPPY.

130. A GOOD DOG DESERVES A GOOD HOME.

131. BEST OF BREED? THAT'S IT?

132. OF COURSE ALL DOGS GO TO HEAVEN. HOW ELSE COULD YOU CALL IT HEAVEN?

133. IF YOU CROSS A DOG WITH A CHICKEN, YOU'LL WIND UP WITH POOCHED EGGS.

134. JUST A LITTLE MORE DOG HUMOR, THERE.

135. GREYHOUNDS CAN RUN AT SPEEDS OF OVER FORTY MILES PER HOUR. WHEN THEY CHASE CARS, THEY MEAN BUSINESS.

136. PEOPLE WILL KNOW
YOUR HEART BY THE
WAY YOU TREAT
YOUR DOG.

137. I CAN'T BELIEVE THAT POODLES COULD ACTUALLY LIKE THOSE HAIRCUTS.

138. NOT EVERY DOG IS A GROWLER - AND NOT EVERY GROWLER IS A DOG.

139. A LEAN DOG SHAMES HIS OWNER.

140. I DON'T CARE WHAT YOU SAY - THE BEDLINGTON TERRIER ISN'T A DOG. IT'S A LAMB.

141. ABRAHAM LINCOLN ONCE SAID, "I CARE NOT FOR A MAN'S RELIGION WHOSE DOG AND CAT ARE NOT THE BETTER FOR IT." I JUST KNOW ABE MADE IT TO HEAVEN.

142. BARK!

143. IF YOU LIE DOWN WITH DOGS, YOU WILL GET UP WITH FLEAS. UNLESS ONE OF US IS WEARING A GOOD FLEA COLLAR.

41

144. THE KOMONDOR WAS THE FIRST CREATURE TO EVER WEAR DREADLOCKS.

145. YOU GONNA EAT THAT?

146. NEVER PASS UP THE CHANCE TO GO FOR A JOYRIDE!

147. WHEN A GOOD DOG HAS A GOOD OWNER, THERE IS NO TELLING WHICH IS HAPPIER.

148. NO ONE APPRECIATES YOUR WISDOM AND GENIUS AS MUCH AS YOUR DOG.

149. AFGHAN HOUNDS DON'T REALLY LIKE TO BE USED AS BLANKETS.

150. IF YOUR DOG DOESN'T LIKE SOME-ONE, YOU CAN BE SURE HE'S GOT A GOOD REASON FOR IT.

151. THE GARBAGE CAN WAS LIKE THAT WHEN I GOT HERE!

152. HONEST!

153. I CAN'T TELL - IS THAT WELSH CORGI LYING DOWN OR STANDING UP?

154. GIVE ME A BREAK - IN HUMAN YEARS, I'M JUST A KID!

155. NEVER GET BETWEEN A DOG AND HIS HYDRANT.

156. DOBERMAN PINSCHERS RARELY PINCH THEIR OWNERS, ALTHOUGH THEY HAVE BEEN KNOWN TO 'GOOSE' THE LADIES FROM TIME TO TIME.

157. YOU CALL "OLD MOTHER HUBBARD" A NURSERY RHYME. WE CALL IT A HORROR STORY!

158. IF YOU WERE HALF AS WONDERFUL AS YOUR DOG THINKS YOU ARE, YOU'D BE A SAINT.

45

159. I PROMISE NOT TO BARK AT THE WIND.

160. FETCH *THIS.*

161. FRENCH BULLDOGS THINK THAT ALL AMERICAN BULLDOGS ARE DUMB.

162. IF YOU DON'T BELIEVE THAT DOGS CAN SMILE, YOU MUST NOT BE MAKING YOUR DOG VERY HAPPY.

163. A COLLIE HAS THE BRAIN OF A MAN AND THE WAYS OF A WOMAN.

164. THE DOG IN "OLD YELLER" WAS NAMED SPIKE, AND WAS BOUGHT AT A POUND FOR THREE DOLLARS. CONSIDERING THE ENDING OF THE MOVIE, MAYBE THEY SHOULD'VE JUST LEFT HIM AT THE POUND.

165. I'LL TRY TO REMEMBER: CRAYONS ARE NOT FOOD.

166. DOGS RARELY WANT TO PLEASE PEOPLE THEY DON'T RESPECT.

167. CONTRARY TO POPULAR BELIEF, SKYE TERRIERS CAN'T ACTUALLY FLY.

168. YOU PEOPLE INVENT WAR, AND YOU THINK DOGS ARE DUMB?

169. HOW WOULD I KNOW HOW ALL MY TOYS GOT STUCK BEHIND THE REFRIGERATOR?

170. THE CANINE GUILT-TRIP: DOGGY EYEBROWS.

171. YOU KNOW YOUR DOG IS IN CHARGE IF HIS WARDROBE IS BIGGER THAN YOURS.

172. THERE IS NO SUCH THING AS A "BAD DOG BONE."

173. A HOUSE WITHOUT A DOG IS NOT A HOME.

49

174. DACHSHUNDS RARELY FALL DOWN. IT'S NOT THAT THEY'RE MORE COORDINATED, THEY JUST DON'T HAVE MUCH FARTHER DOWN TO GO.

175. ARE YOU SURE YOU'RE GONNA EAT THAT?

176. HEY, THROW ME A BONE HERE, WOULD YA?

177. YES! THE PAPERBOY'S HERE!

178. A BATH? AGAIN?

179. HEY, THE SQUIRREL STARTED IT!

180. YOU OWE IT TO ME TO BE WORTHY OF MY DEVOTION.

181. JACK LONDON ONCE SAID, "A BONE TO A DOG IS NOT CHARITY. CHARITY IS THE BONE SHARED WITH THE DOG WHEN YOU ARE JUST AS HUNGRY AS THE DOG."

182. I BET JACK LONDON'S DOG GOT TO SLEEP IN HIS BED WITH HIM!

183. A DALMATIAN CAN'T CHANGE HIS SPOTS.

184. ANOTHER LONG WALK - I'M DOG TIRED!

185. I WASN'T EATING YOUR NEW SHOES. I WAS JUST BREAKING THEM IN FOR YOU.

186. GOD HAS GIVEN DOGS JOY UNTROUBLED. DON'T SCREW IT UP FOR US.

187. BEST OF SHOW? THAT'S IT?

188. OWNERS SHOULDN'T TRY TO MAKE THEIR DOGS PART HUMAN - THEY SHOULD TRY TO MAKE THEMSELVES PART DOG.

53

189. STOP HOUNDING ME!

190. THE CHOW IS NOT MERELY A BREED - IT'S A WAY OF LIFE!

191. DON'T WORRY ABOUT THE RUG... IT ACTUALLY LOOKS LIKE PART OF THE PATTERN.

192. DOGS ARE NEVER FAIR-WEATHER FRIENDS. OUR LOVE FOR OUR OWNERS IS NOT DEPENDENT ON THE CLIMATE OF THEIR LIVES.

193. REMEMBER: WHEN YOU LEAVE THE HOUSE, I MISS YOU. SO HURRY HOME!

194. I'M JUST A WOLF IN DOG'S CLOTHING.

195. I ALWAYS TRY TO LEAVE ROOM IN MY SCHEDULE FOR A GOOD NAP.

196. I'LL TRY TO REMEMBER: YOUR UNDERWEAR IS NOT A TOY.

197. OR FOOD.

198. WHAT? I THOUGHT YOU ENJOYED HUNTING FOR ALL OF THAT STUFF I HIDE UNDER THE BED!

199. IT IS NOT A DOG EAT DOG WORLD. I HAVE NO IDEA HOW THESE CANNIBALISM RUMORS GET STARTED!

200. IF I STARE AT YOU LONG ENOUGH, I'LL GET WHAT I WANT. I THINK WE BOTH KNOW THAT.

201. YOU CAN PUT A SWEATER ON ME WHEN I CAN PUT A TAIL ON YOU.

202. IF DOG PRAYERS WERE ANSWERED, BONES WOULD BE RAINING FROM THE SKY.

57

203. I PROMISE NOT TO BARK AT THE THROW RUG.

204. A DOG IS A MASTER IN SEARCH OF A MASTER WHO ISN'T A DOG.

205. THE CARPET WAS LIKE THAT WHEN I GOT HERE!

206. THE POLICE DOG'S DREAM SUSPECT: THE ROGUE SQUIRREL.

207. IF YOU PUT YOUR DOG ON A SHORT LEASH, YOU'LL BE THE ONLY THING HE CAN PIDDLE ON.

208. YOU PEOPLE INVENT POLITICS, AND YOU THINK DOGS ARE DUMB?

209. IT IS A FALLACY THAT AFGHAN HOUNDS CAN TRACK DOWN COLORFULLY-WOVEN BLANKETS.

210. YOU KNOW YOUR DOG IS IN CHARGE IF YOU SIT ON THE FLOOR BECAUSE THE RECLINER IS *HIS* FAVORITE CHAIR.

211. ANOTHER BATH? WILL I EVER BE CLEAN ENOUGH FOR YOU?

212. HEY, THE CAR STARTED IT!

213. DOES THIS COAT MAKE MY BUTT LOOK BIG?

214. *HOWL!*

215. SCRATCH MY BELLY.

216. OPEN THE DOOR - I WANT OUT AGAIN!

217. OPEN THE DOOR - I WANT IN AGAIN!

218. YOU READ
BIOGRAPHIES,
I SNIFF BUTTS.
PERSONALLY, I DON'T
SEE ANY DIFFERENCE.

61

219. YES, I WAS THE ONE WHO THREW UP IN YOUR NEW SLIPPERS. HEY - AT LEAST I'M HONEST!

220. A FULL-GROWN IRISH WOLFHOUND CAN BE TALLER THAN A MAN, NOT TO MENTION A BETTER COMPANION.

221. A PROBLEM IN THE DOG WORLD: PUPPIES HAVING PUPPIES.

222. HEY! DO I PIDDLE IN YOUR WATER DISH?

223. I WAS BORN WITH MY FUR COAT. WHAT'S YOUR EXCUSE?

224. GOLDEN RETRIEVERS RARELY RETRIEVE GOLD.

225. IF YOU HAVEN'T ROLLED AROUND IN A MUDDY PUDDLE AFTER A SPRING RAIN, YOU JUST HAVEN'T LIVED.

63

226. I SLOBBER, THEREFORE I AM.

227. WELL, YOU NEVER SAID THAT YOU HAD TO READ IT BEFORE I WENT ON THE NEWSPAPER!

228. YES, IT IS A DOG'S LIFE, ACTUALLY.

229. YOU WORK LIKE A DOG? YOU MEAN, YOU HERD SHEEP AROUND ALL DAY?

230. SCRATCH MY BELLY SOME MORE.

231. YOU SLY DOG!

232. THE HAIR OF THE DOG THAT BIT YOU? WELL, NO WONDER HE BIT YOU, IF YOU WERE DRINKING HIS HAIR!

233. WELL, TO BE HONEST, I *AIN'T* NOTHIN' BUT A HOUND DOG.

234. YES! THE GARBAGE MAN'S HERE!

235. RACING DOGS KNOW THOSE RABBITS ARE FAKE. THEY CHASE THEM TO MAKE YOU HAPPY... THEY FIGURE YOU MUST THINK THEY'RE REAL.

236. LET'S GO TO THE PARK!

237. ONE TABLE SCRAP IS WORTH A THOUSAND WORDS.

238. IS THERE SUCH A THING AS POLICE DOG BRUTALITY?

239. I'LL TRY TO REMEMBER: SOAP IS NOT FOOD.

240. BARK, BARK!

241. IF I LAY MY CHIN ON YOUR KNEE AND LOOK REALLY PATHETIC, CAN I HAVE YOUR FOOD?

242. ADULT DOGS HAVE FORTY-TWO TEETH. SO JUST WATCH IT, BUSTER.

243. THE "DOG STAR"? YOU MEAN LASSIE?

244. DOGS CAN'T SEE THE FOREST FOR THE TREES!

245. PAVLOV'S DOGS USED TO SALIVATE AT THE SOUND OF A BELL. THEY EVENTUALLY ALL DROWNED DURING A FOUR-ALARM FIRE.

246. HEY - IT'S NOT LIKE I TOLD YOU TO STEP IN THAT.

247. THERE IS NO SUCH THING AS A "BAD DOG TOY."

248. "SIT PRETTY?" WHAT'S UP WITH THAT?

249. MASTIFFS CAN WEIGH AS MUCH AS 180 POUNDS. VERY FEW OWNERS LET THEM SIT ON THEIR LAPS.

250. YOU'RE GETTING ME A LICENSE? COOL! NOW I CAN DRIVE!

251. HEY, YOU JUST TOLD ME TO FETCH THE NEWSPAPER. YOU DIDN'T SAY ANYTHING ABOUT NOT RIPPING IT TO SHREDS.

252. IN GREEK MYTHOLOGY, A THREE-HEADED DOG NAMED CERBERUS GUARDS THE GATES TO THE UNDERWORLD. I BET HIS BITE IS WORSE THAN HIS BARK!

253. SAINT BERNARDS AREN'T ACTUALLY SAINTS, BUT THERE'S NO TELLING THEM THAT.

254. OKAY, I'LL GIVE YOU MY PAW - BUT I WANT IT RIGHT BACK!

71

255. THOUGH WE DO HAVE FANGS, THERE'S NO SUCH THING AS A VAMPIRE DOG.

256. NO, NOT EVEN BLOODHOUNDS.

257. YOU KNOW YOUR DOG IS IN CHARGE IF YOUR ENTIRE CHRISTMAS LIST CONSISTS OF DOG TOYS.

258. THE BASENJI, AN AFRICAN HOUND, IS THE ONLY DOG THAT CAN'T BARK. DON'T WORRY - I'M SURE THEY'VE FOUND OTHER WAYS TO ANNOY THEIR OWNERS!

259. RUSSIAN SCIENTISTS SENT A SMALL DOG NAMED LAIKA INTO SPACE IN AN ARTIFI-CIAL SATELLITE IN 1957, MAKING HIM THE FIRST DOG TO TRAVEL THAT FAST WITH OUT THE WIND IN HIS FACE.

260. FLORIDA IS FULL OF OLD DOGS WHO SIT IN ROCKING CHAIRS, COMPLAINING ABOUT PUPPIES THESE DAYS.

261. DID I SAY YOU COULD STOP SCRATCHING MY BELLY?

262. THE LHASA APSO USED TO GUARD MONASTERIES IN TIBET, AND THEY WERE OFTEN GIVEN AS GIFTS TO VISITING DIG NITARIES BY THE DALAI LAMA.

263. *BARK BARK BARK BARK BARK BARK BARK BARK BARK!*

264. THE SHAR PEI IS THE ONLY CREATURE ON EARTH THAT GETS LESS WRINKLY WITH AGE.

265. THROW THE STICK!

266. DOGS CAN HEAR NOISES UP TO 250 YARDS AWAY. SO THE NEXT TIME YOU THINK WE'RE BARKING AT NOTHING, YOU'RE PROBABLY STILL RIGHT.

267. FIRST PLACE? THAT'S IT?

268. I PROMISE NOT TO BARK AT THE COUCH CUSHIONS.

269. YOU PEOPLE INVENT NUCLEAR WEAPONS, AND YOU THINK DOGS ARE DUMB?

270. YES! THE METER READER'S HERE!

271. NEVER FEED YOUR DOG CHOCOLATE. NOT ONLY IS IT TOXIC, IT MAKES US BREAK OUT.

272. PANT!

273. I'LL TRY TO REMEMBER: THE NEW PILLOWS ARE NOT FOOD.

274. COME ON - THROW THE STICK AGAIN!

275. I NEVER LET MY TAIL WAG ME.

276. MOST DOGS ACTUAL-
LY HAVE TWO COATS.
THAT'S SO WE CAN
SHED MORE ON YOUR
COUCH.

77

277. YOU'D THINK THE DOGBANE PLANT WOULD BOTHER US, BUT IT DOESN'T.

278. HEY, I'M JUST SHOWING YOUR LEG HOW MUCH I LOVE IT!

279. MY FAVORITE BAND IS THREE DOG NIGHT.

280. "DOWN" MEANS THAT I SHOULD TRY TO JUMP HIGHER AND LICK YOUR FACE, RIGHT?

281. WELL, AT LEAST NOW WE KNOW WHOSE CHRISTMAS TREE THIS IS.

282. BONES THAT SQUEAK ARE JUST PLAIN CREEPY.

283. "NO DOGS ALLOWED"? WHAT KIND OF SICK PLACE IS THIS?

284. TO TRAIN A DOG, YOU NEED TO BE MORE STUBBORN THAN HE IS.

285. GOOD LUCK!

286. WHY DOESN'T MY DOGHOUSE FLY LIKE SNOOPY'S DOES?

287. JUST LOOKING AT A BASSET HOUND MAKES ME WANT TO CRY.

288. YIP!

289. IF YOU DON'T WANT TO PLAY WITH ME, I'LL JUST GO PLAY BY MYSELF. WHERE ARE YOUR NEW SHOES?

290. WHAT FUNNY SMELL?

291. ATTENTION IS A DOG'S GOD-GIVEN RIGHT.

292. AKITAS LOOK LIKE BEARS. THEY EAT LIKE THEM, TOO.

293. YEA! I WON A RIBBON! CAN I EAT IT?

294. MY COUSIN IS CRAZY. HE CHASES PARKED CARS.

295. HASN'T CAUGHT ONE YET.

296. WELL, IF YOU HAVE TO GIVE SOMEONE A FLEA BATH, JUST GIVE IT TO THE FLEAS!

297. YOU CAN'T FOOL ME. I KNOW YOU HID THAT MEDICINE IN MY FOOD.

298. IF YOUR LIFE DOESN'T REVOLVE AROUND ME, SOME THING'S WRONG.

83

299. I'LL TRY TO REMEMBER: ROOF SHINGLES ARE NOT FOOD.

300. IF YOU GO ON VACATION WITHOUT ME, YOU'LL GO INTO DOGGY WITHDRAWAL.

301. I HATE THUNDERSTORMS.

302. YOU KNOW YOUR DOG IS IN CHARGE IF YOU KISS HIM INSTEAD OF YOUR SPOUSE WHEN YOU HEAD OFF TO WORK IN THE MORNING.

303. CHIHUAHUAS MAKE GREAT PETS. IF YOU DON'T WANT A REAL DOG.

304. DON'T LEAVE ME IN THE CAR ON A HOT SUMMER DAY.

305. EVER.

306. THERE IS NOTHING QUITE LIKE A PUPPY.

85

307. SO WE DIDN'T WIN. SO WHAT? I SNIFFED OVER TWO HUNDRED DOGS, YOU GOT A BUFFET-STYLE DINNER, AND I ALMOST BIT MISS CONGENIALITY ON THE RUMP - ALL IN ALL, A GOOD DAY!

308. LET'S GO TO THE PARK AGAIN!

309. I PROMISE NOT TO BARK AT THE REMOTE CONTROL.

310. WANNA BET I CAN'T REACH THAT CHICKEN YOU'RE THAWING FOR DINNER?

311. WHY DO I HAVE TO GO OUTSIDE? YOU GET TO "DO YOUR BUSINESS" IN THE HOUSE!

312. CALL IT A "DOGGY DEN" ALL YOU LIKE - WE BOTH KNOW IT'S A CRATE.

313. WELL, I WOULDN'T DIG UNDER THE FENCE IF YOU JUST GOT RID OF IT, WOULD I?

87

314. TAKE ME FOR A WALK.

315. DO SCHNAUZERS HAVE BEARDS?

317. TOSS THAT FRISBEE OVER HERE, WOULD YOU?

318. I'M NOT DIGGING UP YOUR FLOWER BED, I'M JUST DOING A LITTLE CULTIVATING.

319. DOGS LOVE TO PLAY HIDE AND SEEK.

320. NO, REALLY!

321. I DON'T CARE *WHAT* THAT BOOK OF YOURS SAYS. I WILL NEVER GET ALONG WITH THE CAT.

89

321. IS THAT A BICHON FRISE, OR ARE YOU USING A POWDER PUFF?

322. DOGS WILL BE DOGS!

323. SURE, YOU CAN NAME ME "CUDDLE POO." YOU'RE THE ONE THAT'S GONNA HAVE TO CALL FOR ME IN FRONT OF THE NEIGHBORS.

324. ALL WORK AND NO PLAY MAKES FIDO A DULL DOG.

356. HEY, DON'T I GET A CHRISTMAS STOCKING, TOO?

326. YOU PEOPLE INVENT TOXIC WASTE, AND YOU THINK DOGS ARE DUMB?

327. THE HAPPIEST DOG HAS NOT A MASTER, BUT A FRIEND.

328. I'LL TRY TO REMEMBER: YOUR SUN GLASSES ARE NOT A TOY.

329. TAKE ME FOR A WALK AGAIN!

330. I DON'T WANT DOG FOOD – I WANT PEOPLE FOOD!

331. I KNOW I ATE YOUR HOMEWORK, BUT YOUR TEACHER'S NEVER GOING TO BELIEVE YOU.

332. DO POODLES GET PERMS?

333. DRUG-SNIFFING DOGS MUST REALLY LOVE THEIR JOB.

334. *YOU ONLY THINK YOU'RE THE ALPHA MALE IN THIS PACK.*

93

335. LET'S GO TO THE PET STORE!

336. YOU WANT ME TO "PLAY DEAD"? SURE DOESN'T SOUND LIKE A FUN GAME TO ME!

337. I WILL PROTECT YOU.

338. BARKING DOGS NEVER BITE - UNTIL THEY STOP BARKING.

339. OLD ENGLISH SHEEP DOGS ARE COOL - BUT HOW DO THEY SEE THROUGH ALL THAT HAIR?

340. IT'S EASIER TO GET A TOY AWAY FROM A CHILD THAN A PUPPY.

341. DOGS AND CATS BOTH HAVE CLAWS, BUT WE CAN'T RETRACT OURS LIKE THEY CAN. WE CAN'T EVEN FIGURE OUT WHY THEY'D WANT TO.

342. CAN WE GO TO A PARK THAT HAS ROLLER COASTERS THIS TIME?

343. I'M NOT A MUTT – I'M A MONGREL!

344. YOU KNOW YOUR DOG IS IN CHARGE IF YOU DECIDE TO HAVE KIDS JUST SO YOUR DOG WILL HAVE SOMEONE TO PLAY WITH.

345. IS IT JUST ME, OR DO BOSTON TERRIERS LOOK LIKE THEIR EYES ARE GONNA POP OUT OF THEIR HEADS?

346. THERE'S A PLANT CALLED THE DOGTOOTH VIOLET, WHICH DOESN'T LOOK ANYTHING LIKE A DOG'S TOOTH, AND ISN'T EVEN A VIOLET. YOU PEOPLE ARE WEIRD.

347. DOESN'T A MEXICAN HAIRLESS GET COLD?

348. YOU JUST STAND THERE WHILE WE PULL THE SLED - AND YOU GET THE MONEY IF WE WIN? SOMETHING'S NOT RIGHT HERE.

97

349. MINIATURE PINSCHERS THINK THEY'RE TOUGH.

350. THEY'RE WRONG.

351. OF COURSE YOU CAN PUT ME ON A LEASH WHEN WE GO RUNNING... IF YOU LIKE BEING DRAGGED ALONG THE SIDE WALK ON YOUR FACE.

352. DOGS USUALLY BECOME FULLY GROWN AT EIGHT MONTHS TO TWO YEARS OF AGE. POMERANIANS ARE FULL-GROWN IN ABOUT THREE DAYS.

353. I KNOW I'M NOT A SAINT BERNARD, BUT CAN I HAVE ONE OF THOSE KEGS OF BRANDY ANYWAY?

354. IF YOU FEED ME FROM YOUR PLATE, I'LL LET YOU EAT OUT OF MY BOWL!

355. WHAT, EXACTLY, IS A LABRADOR, AND HOW DOES ONE GO ABOUT RETRIEVING IT?

356. GROWL.

357. WHEN I GET TO HEAVEN, WILL GOD LET ME GET UP ON HIS COUCH?

358. SCREEN DOORS MAKE AN EXCELLENT BRAKING SYSTEM.

359. POTTED PLANTS GROW BETTER IF I LIE ON THEM.

360. THEY GROW EVEN BETTER IF I EAT THEM.

361. SOME HOUND HUNT BY SCENT, OTHERS HUNT BY SIGHT. I PREFER TO USE MY INTUITION.

362. DON'T WORRY - I'M SURE SOMEDAY I'LL RECOGNIZE THE WORD "NO" AS WELL AS I RECOGNIZE THE WORD "BACON."

101

363. ARE THERE DOGS ON OTHER PLANETS?

364. OF COURSE I CAN FIT THROUGH THE FENCE! JUST WATCH!

365. UH... MY HEAD'S STUCK.

366. PEOPLE PUT ON COLOGNE, THEN THEY DON'T EVEN BOTHER TO SNIFF EACH OTHER ON THE STREET. WHAT'S THE POINT?

367. DINING ROOM TABLES SHOULD HAVE ON-RAMPS.

368. THE DOGS ON TV AREN'T REAL? SO, ARE YOU SAYING I SHOULDN'T BARK AT THEM NON-STOP?

369. IF A DOG BARKS HIS HEAD OFF IN THE FOREST AND NO HUMANS ARE AROUND TO HEAR HIM, IS HE STILL A "BAD DOG"?

103

370. BUT I THOUGHT WE WERE BOTH SUPPOSED TO GET WET WHEN YOU GIVE ME A BATH!

371. LESS SPAGHETTI, MORE MEATBALLS.

372. DOGS LOVE WHEN IT SNOWS. NOT ONLY IS IT FUN TO PLAY IN, BUT THERE'S ALWAYS THAT CHANCE THAT OBEDIENCE SCHOOL WILL BE CLOSED.

373. I WILL OBEY YOU.

374. EVENTUALLY.

375. SO YOU DON'T LIKE TO PLAY THE CHASING GAME IN THE MIDDLE OF A BUSY STREET?

376. YOU KNOW YOUR DOG IS IN CHARGE IF YOU HAVE MORE PICTURES OF HIM IN YOUR WALLET THAN ANY OTHER FAMILY MEMBER.

377. I'D LOOK A LOT LESS PATHETIC IF YOU'D STOP WHAT-EVER YOU'RE DOING AND PET ME.

105

378. YOU CALL IT AN "INFESTATION." I CALL IT A "BUFFET."

379. I HAVE NO IDEA HOW ALL OF THAT DOG HAIR GOT INTO THE NEIGHBOR'S KIDDY POOL.

380. OOH! LOOK AT THE PRETTY CLAW MARKS ON YOUR BRAND NEW CAR!

381. I'LL TRY TO REMEMBER: CREDIT CARDS ARE NOT FOOD.

382. WELL, YOU DON'T EXACTLY SMELL LIKE A BED OF ROSES YOURSELF, YOU KNOW.

383. YOU DON'T WANT ME TO STEAL YOUR UNDERWEAR? SO I GUESS WEARING THEM ON MY HEAD IS OUT, TOO, RIGHT?

384. BUT THE DRYER IS THE PERFECT PLACE TO STORE MY SLOBBERY TOYS!

385. SORRY I TRIPPED YOU. WOULD IT MAKE YOU FEEL BETTER IF I SLOBBER ON YOUR FACE?

386. NO ONE SAID YOU HAD TO DRAG ME ALL THE WAY HOME. YOU COULD'VE JUST STAYED AT THE PARK WITH ME ALL DAY.

387. WHY ARE THERE CARS NAMED AFTER CATS, BUT NO CARS NAMED AFTER DOGS?

388. I'M NOT STUCK IN THE SINK. I JUST DON'T FEEL LIKE MOVING.

389. IS IT TRUE THAT DOGS AREN'T ALLOWED IN RESTAURANTS BECAUSE WE CAN'T FIGURE OUT WHAT NOT TO ORDER? OR IS IT JUST THAT CARPET THING AGAIN?

390. CHEWING UP THE ALUMINUM SIDING ANNOYS YOU?

391. OKAY, SO MAYBE DUNKING THE CAT IN MY WATER DISH WASN'T A GOOD IDEA.

392. YOU KNOW, YOU'D PROBABLY BE ABLE TO KEEP UP WITH ME IF YOU USED ALL FOUR LEGS INSTEAD OF JUST THOSE TWO.

393. OH, COME ON – THE NEIGHBORS LOVE IT WHEN I "PLAY RABID"!

394. LET'S PLAY FRISBEE AGAIN!

395. YOU DON'T WANT ME TO SNIFF YOUR CROTCH, YOU DON'T WANT ME TO SNIFF YOUR BUTT – WHAT EXACTLY DO YOU WANT?

396. OKAY, THE NEXT TIME YOU'RE WATCHING A SCARY MOVIE, I WON'T STARE AT SOMETHING INVISIBLE IN A DARK CORNER OF THE ROOM AND GROWL.

397. A BATH? BUT I JUST WENT SWIMMING IN THE DUCK POND!

398. YOU PEOPLE INVENT TAXES, AND YOU THINK DOGS ARE DUMB?

399. I HAVE TO CHASE SQUIRRELS! IT'S MY JOB!

400. DOGS REFUSE TO BELIEVE IN REINCAR
NATION. WE'RE TOO AFRAID THAT WE'LL
COME BACK AS A CAT.

401. OR A MAILMAN.

402. I THOUGHT I WAS SUPPOSED TO BE
YOUR ALARM CLOCK!

403. WELL, WHY DO YOU CALL THIS CAT
THING A LITTER BOX IF I CAN'T HAVE
MY PUPPIES IN IT?

404. DROOLING ON COMPANY IS AN IMPOR-
TANT SOCIAL SKILL.

405. THROW THE BALL!

406. OKAY, FIVE MINUTES STARING AT A BOOK IS LONG ENOUGH. NOW PAY ATTENTION TO ME AGAIN!

113

406. I WASN'T STEALING YOUR SOCKS, I WAS JUST KEEPING THEM SAFE.

407. AND WET.

408. I MEAN IT - THE TELEPHONE IS EVIL!

409. I TRY NOT TO ROLL IN ANYTHING THAT SMELLS WORSE THAN I DO.

410. SO, HERDING THE MARATHON RUNNERS ISN'T A GOOD THING?

411. WOULD ONE OF YOU MIND HITTING THAT PING-PONG BALL OVER THIS WAY? I'M GETTING TIRED OF RUNNING FROM ONE END OF THE TABLE TO THE OTHER!

412. WHY CAN'T I SIT ON YOUR LAP WHILE YOU'RE DRIVING?

413. YOU KNOW THOSE TULIP BULBS YOU BURIED IN THE BACK YARD? THEY WERE DELICIOUS!

414. WELL, IF I GET UNDER YOUR FEET WHILE YOU'RE CARRYING GROCERIES, I HAVE A BETTER CHANCE OF GETTING THE FOOD BEFORE IT GETS TO THE FRIDGE.

415. SO THAT THING I BURIED IN THE NEIGHBOR'S BACK YARD WAS YOUR CHECKBOOK?

416. WHAT'S A CHECKBOOK?

417. SORRY, BUT I CAN ONLY WALK ONE FOOT AN HOUR. ESPECIALLY WHEN YOU'RE IN A HURRY

418. I'LL TRY TO REMEMBER: TOOTHPASTE IS NOT FOOD.

419. I WILL NEVER LEAVE YOUR SIDE.

117

421. OKAY, SO BEGGING YOU TO TAKE ME FOR A RUN AND THEN STEALING YOUR SNEAKERS MAY BE COUNTER-PRODUCTIVE.

422. THROW THE BALL AGAIN!

423. "COME!" MEANS THAT I HAVE TO GO TO YOU? ARE YOU SURE IT ISN'T THE OTHER WAY AROUND?

424. I DO NOT PRETEND MY COLLAR IS TOO TIGHT EVERY TIME A STRANGER WALKS BY.

425. OKAY - I PROMISE THAT'S THE LAST TIME I'LL DRINK YOUR BEER AND START A DRUNKEN BRAWL WITH MY FOOD DISH.

426. HEY, AT LEAST I'M UNIQUE. MOST DOGS WOULD WAIT UNTIL YOU TAKE YOUR SHOES OFF BEFORE THEY CHEW ON THEM.

427. THE ONLY THINGS BIGGER THAN A DOG'S HEART ARE HIS LUNGS.

428. YOU KNOW YOUR DOG IS IN CHARGE IF YOU RARELY SOCIALIZE, BUT YOU LET YOUR DOGS HAVE HIS FRIENDS OVER EVERY DAY.

429. DOGS AND GUYS ARE A LOT ALIKE. WE BOTH HAVE A FEAR OF VACUUM CLEANERS, WE'RE BOTH SUSPICIOUS OF THE MAILMAN, AND NEITHER OF US NOTICES WHEN A WOMAN GETS A HAIRCUT.

430. WHIMPER.

431. IF YOU DON'T LIKE POLICE DOGS, THE NEXT TIME YOU'RE IN TROUBLE, TRY CALLING A CAT.

432. OH... THAT'S THE COMPUTER PLUG?

433. YOU REALLY SHOULDN'T SWEAR LIKE THAT, YOU KNOW.

434. NO, ACTUALLY, I DON'T RECALL YOUR TELLING ME TO GET OFF THE BED EVERY SINGLE DAY FOR THE PAST TWO YEARS. WHY?

121

435. I DON'T CARE WHAT YOU SAY – THAT FEATHER DUSTER IS MY MORTAL ENEMY.

436. I KNOW I'M NOT SUPPOSED TO DIG UP THE LAWN. THAT'S WHY I DUG UP THE NEIGHBOR'S LAWN.

437. WELL, I DIDN'T KNOCK YOU DOWN ON PURPOSE!

438. I'LL TRY TO REMEMBER: YOUR BRA IS NOT FOOD.

439. LET'S GO FOR A RUN!

440. HEY – IT'S MY DUTY TO ROOT THROUGH ALL OF YOUR GUESTS' COATS AND PURSES.

441. SLIDING GLASS DOORS ARE JUST YOUR WAY OF GETTING REVENGE FOR THE CARPETS, AREN'T THEY?

442. WHAT MUDDY PAW PRINTS?

443. I DON'T LIKE THE INTERNET. THERE AREN'T ANY EMOTICONS FOR TAIL-WAGGING.

444. WHAT'S WRONG WITH DOING THIS WITH MY STUFFED ANIMAL IN FRONT OF COMPANY?

445. WHAT? I THOUGHT YOUR DATE WOULD WANT TO SEE YOUR DIRTY UNDERWEAR, ESPECIALLY HANGING FROM MY MOUTH AND COVERED WITH DROOL!

446. YES, I'M IN THE DRYER. WHY? WHERE WAS I SUPPOSED TO BE?

447. ARE YOU SURE THERE AREN'T ANY SHARKS IN THIS BATHTUB?

448. I WONDER IF BIRD DOGS EVER GET CONFUSED ABOUT WHETHER THEY'RE A BIRD OR A DOG?

449. I PROMISE NOT TO BARK AT THE CAR RADIO.

450. WELL, I WOULDN'T GET MY HEAD STUCK IN THE BLINDS IF YOU REMEMBERED TO PULL THEM UP IN THE MORNING!

451. LET'S GO FOR ANOTHER RUN!

452. SOME SAY THAT DOGS TURN AROUND BEFORE LYING DOWN BECAUSE WILD DOGS TRAMPLE THE GRASS WHERE THEY'RE GOING TO LIE, AND IT'S SOME DEEP-ROOTED, PSYCHOLOGICAL, GENETIC, INSTINCTIVE THING.

453. WE BOTH KNOW IT'S JUST BECAUSE DOGS ARE CRAZY.

454. I'LL TRY TO REMEMBER: TOILET PAPER IS NOT A TOY.

455. DOGS NEVER PRETEND. IF THEY DON'T LIKE YOU, YOU'LL KNOW IT.

456. WAS THAT THE CAN OPENER?

457. THE NAME "ROVER" BECAME POPULAR FOR DOGS AFTER THE FIRST CANINE STAR MADE AN APPEARANCE IN 1905, IN A SILENT FILM CALLED "RESCUED BY ROVER." DOGS THE WORLD OVER REGARD THIS AS ONE OF THE GREAT TRAGEDIES OF THE TWENTIETH CENTURY.

458. LOOK! THE GARBAGE MAN'S STEALING ALL OUR STUFF AGAIN!

459. I DIDN'T KNOW THAT WAS THE JUDGE'S LEG.

460. DOGS WOULD HAVE BUILT A VAST, COMPLEX CIVILIZATION LIKE MAN DID, BUT THEN WE FIGURED OUT THAT WE COULD LICK OURSELVES.

461. NO MATTER WHERE WE LIVE, JUST REMEMBER - I OWN IT.

462. IF IT AIN'T COLD, WET, AND SLOPPY, IT AIN'T A REAL KISS!

463. ARE YOU SURE THERE AREN'T ANY LEFT OVERS IN BETWEEN THE COUCH CUSHIONS?

464. SORRY, BUT I HAVE TO FIND JUST THE RIGHT SPOT! THESE THINGS TAKE TIME!

465. YOU'RE JUST JEALOUS BECAUSE I CAN SCRATCH MYSELF IN PUBLIC WITHOUT GETTING ALL EMBARRASSED.

466. I WAS A DOG YESTERDAY. I'M A DOG TODAY. I'LL BE A DOG TOMORROW. THERE'S SO LITTLE ROOM FOR ADVANCEMENT!

467. THEN AGAIN, WHAT COULD BE BETTER THAN BEING A DOG?

468. WHEN HE'S GOT A GOOD OWNER, EVEN WHEN A DOG'S WHINING, HE'S HAPPY.

469. I COULD HAVE SWORN I HEARD THE CAN OPENER.

470. RUFF!

471. I HAVE NO IDEA HOW ALL OF THAT DOG HAIR GOT INTO THE HOT TUB.

472. DOGS ARE DOGS. THERE'S REALLY NOT MUCH MORE TO IT THAN THAT!

473. IT ISN'T TRUE THAT DOGS SWEAT THROUGH THEIR TONGUES. WE ACTUALLY SWEAT THROUGH THE PADS OF OUR FEET. WE JUST PANT TO GET SLOBBER ALL OVER YOU.

474. OKAY, YOU CAN GO FOR A WALK - I'M STILL GOING FOR A RUN!

475. WHY IS IT THAT YOU NEVER SEE A SIGN THAT SAYS "BEWARE OF DOG" AROUND A POODLE'S HOUSE?

476. THE BIGGER THE PUDDLE OF DROOL, THE GREATER THE LOVE OF THE ONE WHO CREATED IT.

477. TO PEOPLE, THE WORD "PET" IS OFTEN A NOUN. TO US, IT'S ALWAYS A VERB.

478. I KNOW IT'S 3:00 A.M., BUT I REALLY DO HAVE TO GO OUT RIGHT NOW!

479. YEAH, I KNOW MY HIND LEG IS OUT OF CONTROL. WHAT OF IT?

480. I NEVER MET A PIT BULL I DIDN'T PRETEND TO LIKE.

481. BIG DOGS MAKE THE BEST PILLOWS.

482. ACCIDENTALLY STEPPING ON A SHAR-PEI IS KIND OF LIKE SLIPPING ON A BANANA PEEL.

483. IT'S ACTUALLY A POLICE DOG'S JOB TO CHASE CARS. IS THAT COOL, OR WHAT?

484. THE PARK IS THE BEST PLACE TO CATCH UP ON DOG GOSSIP.

485. ARE YOU SURE THAT WASN'T THE CAN OPENER?

486. DOGS NEVER PRETEND. IF THEY LOVE YOU, YOU'LL KNOW IT.

487. I KNOW IT'S 3:07 A.M., BUT I REALLY DO HAVE TO COME BACK IN RIGHT NOW!

488. DOGS SPEND ALL OF OUR TIME SLEEPING, EATING, AND PLAY-ING, BECAUSE THESE ARE THE THINGS WE DO BEST!

489. YOU KNOW, I WOULDN'T HAVE TO DRAG MY TOYS BACK INTO THE MIDDLE OF THE ROOM IF YOU'D JUST LEAVE THEM THERE IN THE FIRST PLACE!

490. YES, ACTUALLY, I DO THINK IT'S A GOOD IDEA TO BARK AT THE SNOWMAN IN OUR FRONT YARD FOR THREE STRAIGHT HOURS. WHY?

491. HEY - WHERE'D THE SNOWMAN GO?

492. DOGS ARE LOYAL, HONEST, AND COURA GEOUS. THE ONLY THING THAT KEEPS US FROM BEING BOY SCOUTS IS THAT WE'RE NEVER "PREPARED" FOR THINGS LIKE THE DOORBELL.

493. BESIDES, WE LOOK SILLY IN THOSE LITTLE SHORTS.

494. GEE... I HAVE NO IDEA HOW YOUR LIP STICK GOT EATEN BY ME.

139

495. I WILL DO MY PART TO MAKE OUR HOUSE A HOME.

496. "KIBBLE" ACTUALLY TASTES BETTER THAN IT SOUNDS.

497. I WONDER IF DOGFISH EVER GET CONFUSED ABOUT WHETHER THEY'RE A DOG OR A FISH?

498. DOGS ARE ACTUALLY NUMBER FIVE ON THE LIST OF SMARTEST ANIMALS ON THE EARTH.

499. FIVE AND A HALF, IF YOU COUNT HUMANS.

500. I REALLY DO LOVE YOU, YOU KNOW.

141